Simply Smoked

A LITTLE BOOK OF TEMPTING RECIPES FOR SMOKED FISH, MEAT AND VEGETABLES

GEORGE DORGAN

ILLUSTRATIONS BY MADELEINE DAVID

GRUB STREET · LONDON

Published by Grub Street
The Basement, 10 Chivalry Road, London SW 11 1HT

Copyright © Grub Street 1996
Text copyright © George Dorgan 1996
Illustrations by Madeleine David

British Library Cataloguing in Publication Data
Dorgan, George
Simply Smoked: Little Book of Tempting Recipes for Smoked
Fish, Meat and Vegetables – (Simply Series)
I. Title II. David, Madeleine III. Series
641.5
ISBN 1-898697-29-9

Colour origination by Modern Age Repro, Hong Kong
Printed and bound in Italy

CONTENTS

INTRODUCTION

Smoked foods were an important, early breakthrough in the course of human civilisation. The smoking method allowed people to preserve plentiful foods for a time of scarcity and even though we now have refrigeration, smoked foods are still enjoyed for their taste and texture.

Before refrigeration, meat and fish were heavily smoked for weeks – even months – and came out with almost no moisture content, so they could be safely kept for many months at room temperature. Red herring is a good example of pre-refrigeration smoking, a fish that is so hard it could seriously hurt someone if you hit them with it. Careful smoking still does preserve food and smoked salmon keeps much longer than fresh, but it must still be refrigerated.

This book is NOT about how to smoke foods at home. Although good hot-smoked foods can be made at home with much practice, a home-smoker cannot produce the kind of silken cold-smoked salmon people love so much. Smoking is – in the end – much like wine making, something best left to experts.

The suppliers listed in this book are artisan smokeries such as Minola Smoked Products in Gloucestershire. The smokery is run by Hugh and Jane Forestier-Walker and is honestly not much to look at. All there is to see is a collection of wooden sheds – the smokehouses – with a firebox on the floor stuffed with burning oak logs. This produces the smoke that wafts up and works its marvel of subtly altering the taste and texture of the foods being smoked.

There are a host of variables the smoker must take into account. The moisture content of most foods must be reduced before smoking. This is done by brining and can be either dry (in salt only) or wet (in a salt solution which can be flavoured with herbs and spices). Air temperature and humidity affect smoking, both how long something must be smoked and if smoking can be done at all. A specific internal temperature must be achieved and modern technology helps here as most good smokers use temperature probes. The smoker must also consider the type of food being smoked and what kind of product is desired.

There are two basic, different smoking methods, hot and cold. Cold smoking produces the characteristic silky texture in fishes like salmon and trout and is done at a temperature less than 30°C (86°F). Cold-smoked meats must be cooked before eating, although fish doesn't have to be, and the smoking is done to add flavour. Hot-smoked foods are produced at temperatures usually over 80°C (176°F) and hot-smoked fishes must achieve an internal temperature of 64°C (147°F). Hot-smoked foods – like chicken or turkey – taste "cooked" because they are.

Concern has been expressed in some quarters over the possible carcinogenic content of smoked foods. Research on smoking foods has been conducted since 1929 at what is now known as the CSL Food Science Laboratory, Torry in Aberdeen. Their examination of the carcinogenic content of smoked foods is quite interesting and very reassuring. The wood burning process, they say, produces a complex group of compounds known collectively as PNEHs. These are also present in natural fossil fuels as well as smoked foods and fruits and vegetables. According to Torry spokesman Alan Hume" the natural levels of these compounds are much higher in lettuce and asparagus than in smoked foods". He was also able to shed some light on the issue of which type of wood is best suited for smoking foods. "When you use soft woods you get changes in flavour in the final product - acrid caramelised flavours. Using hardwoods you get softer, more smoke-like flavours."

Smoked foods are more widely available than ever before and most supermarkets stock a wide range. Read labels carefully and look for words like "oak smoked", as oak is generally acknowledged as the best wood for smoking. If the label says "smoked over oak logs," so much the better, because then the wood is identifiable whereas sawdust could come from any kind of wood. Good smokeries in Scotland, however, may use chippings from whisky barrels for smoking and this also gives a quality product. The colour of smoked foods should be appealing to look at; the lurid yellow colour of some smoked haddock comes from a food dye. Texture should be firm, not mushy or hard. Beware of "bargain" prices as you may be buying a vastly inferior product, indifferently smoked – if at all – over sawdust; many foods, like "smoked" cheeses, are merely smeared with chemical smoke. Cheeses that have been naturally smoked have criss-crossing lines that show where the cheese rested on a rack during the smoking process.

As many of the products may be unfamiliar to most people, I thought it would be useful to include information on pairing smoked foods with drinks. The results have been quite surprising. Light red wines, for instance, often went better with fish than white wines did. And some drinks that are not thought to partner foods well were the most enjoyable with smoked foods, especially Spanish Sherry, German wines and single malt whiskies. For each ingredient, I have listed the range of drinks that go well with it. I have also listed drinks that went especially well with certain recipes whenever possible. These are indicated in each case by the glass symbol.

Finally, I would like to thank the chefs and suppliers who have contributed to this book, for their time, effort and generosity. I would also like to thank the national wine promoting organisations that arranged tastings for this book: the Australian Wine Bureau, Food and Wine from France, Food and Wine from Spain, the German Wine Information Service, United Distillers, the Wine Institute of California, and Wines of South Africa.

George Dorgan

SMOKED SALMON

Smoked salmon is a wonderful ingredient and is the classic smoked food of all time. Like all smoked foods it is delicious eaten on its own and a smoked salmon sandwich is rarely refused at afternoon tea. But too often smoked salmon is treated reverentially because it is seen as a luxury food. This is a shame because it is now at a price in super-markets which makes it possible to use more frequently, and its strong flavour comes through any number of interesting treatments. Namita Punjabi of Chutney Mary's restaurant in London serves it on warm naan bread, sprinkled with onion and coriander chutney. She uses smoked salmon in a three-layered kedgeree, using plain rice, a red rice flavoured with a red chilli pickle and a green rice with coriander and onion chutney.

Smoked salmon trimmings are about a quarter of the price of sliced salmon and are widely available. Many of the recipes in this book use trimmings, so they are not expensive dishes. You might think of using smoked salmon in pasta dishes; processed with cream cheese for sandwich and bagel spreads; as a filling for jacket potatoes with soured cream; or in a Salad Niçoise instead of tuna. Use the skin of smoked salmon for roasting a large piece of fish in the same way you would use bacon for roasting a joint; the flavour really penetrates through the fish.

Fino Quinta sherry by Osborne is best; French Anjou Blanc; German Spatburgunder (Pinot Noir), dry Muller-Thurgau from Mosel Saar Ruwer, mature Riesling from the Pfalz; unoaked Australian Chardonnay; South African Gewurztraminer; or a Lowland or Speyside single malt whisky.

MILLE-FEUILLE OF SMOKED SALMON

From the Scottish Salmon Smokers Association, developed by the Gleneagles Hotel

INGREDIENTS

8	sheets filo pastry, 175g (6 oz)
50g (2 oz)	melted butter
100g (3½ oz)	smoked salmon trimmings
100ml (3½ fl.oz)	double cream
1	bunch chives, roughly chopped
	salt and pepper
1 tsp	chopped dill
250g (8 oz)	soured cream
12	large slices smoked salmon
2	limes
4	sprigs frisée lettuce

METHOD

Using a 7.5cm (3") cutter, cut the filo into 24 rounds. Lay 12 rounds on a greased baking sheet, brush with melted butter and top with another 12 rounds and brush these with butter as well. Bake in a hot oven, 220°C, 425°F, Gas Mark 7 for 5 minutes until golden. Allow to cool.

Finely mix salmon trimmings and double cream in a food processor. Add chives, salt and pepper and mix again.

Mix dill and soured cream, adding a bit of water if necessary to make a thin sauce.

Cut the salmon slices with the same 7.5cm (3") cutter, allowing 3 rounds per portion. Alternate layers of pastry, creamed salmon and smoked salmon, repeating twice more and finishing with smoked salmon rounds on top, making 4 rounds. "Brand" in crosshatches with a red hot needle or skewer and allow to chill in the refrigerator. Garnish with half a lime placed on the frisée lettuce sprig and pour a bit of sauce on the plate.

Serves 4

℞ *Pinot Noir from California*

SMOKED SALMON MOUSSE

From Peter Dodd, chef, Wig & Mitre, Lincoln

INGREDIENTS

200g (7 oz)	smoked salmon trimmings
200ml (7 fl.oz)	double cream
200ml (7 fl.oz)	whipping cream
100ml (3½ fl.oz)	water
	lemon juice, to taste

METHOD

Put the salmon in a food processor and mix until smooth, adding only as much water as required for a workable consistency. Chill 20-30 minutes. Return to processor and add double cream and lemon juice. Chill another 20-30 minutes. In a mixing bowl whip up whipping cream then fold into the salmon mix. Refrigerate for 1 hour.

TO SERVE

This mousse can be used to fill lined moulds, or piped into tartlets as a canape. The Wig & Mitre often serves it as part of a smoked salmon parcel, lining dariole moulds with smoked salmon, filled with mousse and left to chill in the refrigerator.

Serves 8 as an appetiser

℞ *Unoaked California Chardonnay, Anjou Blanc from France.*

CHILLED SUMMER VEGETABLE SOUP WITH SMOKED SALMON

From Alan Jefferson-Mackney, chef, Winterbourne Arms, Winterbourne, Berks

INGREDIENTS

250g (8 oz)	smoked salmon trimmings, diced
500g (1 lb)	blanched, skinned, seeded and diced tomatoes
1	10cm (4") length of cucumber, diced
2	shredded spring onions
¼	diced red pepper
¼	diced yellow pepper
10	sliced and blanched French beans
450ml (¾ pt)	light fish stock
6	sliced and blanched mangetout
1	stick celery, sliced
2	crushed garlic cloves
2 tbs	olive oil
1 tsp	chopped chives
1 tsp	chopped basil
	salt and pepper to taste

METHOD

Mix all ingredients together and marinate one day before use.

Serves 6

♀ *Pinot Gris from Alsace.*

CHARGRILLED SMOKED SALMON WITH SWEET PEPPERS AND LIME

From David Lewis, chef, The Feathers Hotel, Woodstock, Oxon.

INGREDIENTS

THE DRESSING

2	red peppers, deseeded and quartered
2	yellow peppers, deseeded and quartered
8 tbs	olive oil
1	clove garlic, chopped
2 tbs	white wine vinegar
6	large basil leaves, chopped salt and freshly ground black pepper
250g (8 oz)	smoked salmon, in 4 slices fresh chervil and dill lime segments for garnish

METHOD

Preheat the grill to its highest setting. Place pepper quarters skin side up and grill until skin begins to bubble. Remove and place in covered bowl for 10 minutes.

Peel the peppers and trim the ends so that you have 16 neat rectangles. Place the discarded skin and trimmings into a food processor along with the olive oil, chopped garlic and white wine vinegar. Purée until smooth then pass through a fine sieve, add the basil and season to taste.

Cut the peppers into fine strips and marinate in the dressing 6-8 hours.

Divide the peppers and dressing on to 4 plates. Lightly oil the smoked salmon and chargrill very quickly so as not to over cook the salmon, just marking it for flavour.

Lay the chargrilled salmon on top of the peppers. Garnish with lime segments and fresh chervil and dill.

Serves 4

♀ *Pinot Noir from Alsace (chilled) or California.*

SMOKED SALMON WITH MUSSELS WARMED IN BASIL BUTTER

From Alan Jefferson-Mackney, chef, Winterbourne Arms, Winterbourne, Berks.

INGREDIENTS

250g (8 oz)	sliced smoked salmon

SALAD

¼	fine curly endive (frisée)
¼	lollo rosso
Mix of:	bok choy
	rocket
	rhubarb chard
	mustard chard
	lamb's lettuce (mâche)
	young dandelion greens
4 tbs	olive oil
	salt and pepper
40	mussels blanched and removed from their shells

BASIL BUTTER

1 bunch	basil processed with
50g (2 oz)	butter
4	blanched, peeled, seeded and diced tomatoes
4	lemon wedges (or more)

Arrange the sliced salmon on four plates leaving space for the mussels. Dress the salad with olive oil, salt and pepper. Arrange on top of the salmon.

Warm the mussels in the basil butter. When warm add the diced tomato. Place the mussels on the plate and serve with a lemon wedge.

Serves 4

♀ *Pinot Gris from Alsace.*

BAKED SMOKED SALMON ROULADE

From Marion Mann, Teviot Game Fare Smokery, Kelso, Roxburghshire

I N G R E D I E N T S

ROULADE

4	eggs, separated
100ml (3½ fl.oz)	fromage frais
100ml (3½ fl.oz)	whipping cream
	pinch of chopped dill
	squeeze of lemon juice
	salt and pepper

FILLING

250g (8 oz)	smoked salmon trimmings
125g (4 oz)	finely chopped boiled onion
2 tbs	mayonnaise
	pinch of chopped dill
	squeeze of lemon juice
	salt and pepper

M E T H O D

Place egg yolks, fromage frais, whipping cream, dill, lemon juice and seasoning in bowl or food processor and whisk thoroughly. Whisk egg whites until stiff. Thoroughly mix in ¼ of the whites into the yolk mixture, then carefully fold in remaining whites. Line a Swiss roll tin with greaseproof paper and pour in mixture. Bake at 180°C, 350°F, Gas Mark 4 for approximately 10 minutes.

Mix smoked salmon trimmings, onion, mayonnaise, dill, lemon juice and season.

When roulade is cooked remove from oven and allow to cool. Turn out on to a sheet of greaseproof or a tea towel. Remove greaseproof from top. Spread filling and roll from short side. Slice and serve with a green salad and lemon slice.

Serves 4-6

♀ *Anjou Blanc from France.*

SMOKED SALMON SOUP

From Mike Wamersley, chef, The Three Lions, Stuckton, Fordingbridge, Hants.

INGREDIENTS	
2	onions
6	shallots
½	bulb fennel
2	carrots
2	celery sticks
2	leeks
50g (2 oz)	butter
1.5 kg (3 lb)	smoked salmon trimmings
1	bottle Chardonnay

bouquet garni consisting of:
20	white peppercorns
1	star anise

1	handful herb stalks – parsley, chervil, tarragon, dill
2	thyme sprigs
1	bayleaf
	(all wrapped in muslin)
$3\frac{1}{2}$ litres (6 pt)	fish stock (or water if not available)
300ml ($\frac{1}{2}$ pint)	double cream
	chopped chives

METHOD

Sweat half the vegetables in 25g (1 oz) butter for 5 minutes in a covered pan, without browning. Sauté the other half in a separate pan in another 25g (1 oz) butter for 5 minutes and reserve. Keep a small amount of smoked salmon trimmings for garnish and add the rest to pan with sweated vegetables and sweat for 2 minutes. Add white wine and bouquet garni. Reduce by half. Add fish stock or water and simmer 25 minutes. Strain. Add reserved vegetables and cook a further 15 minutes. Add 300ml ($\frac{1}{2}$ pt) double cream. Simmer 5 minutes.

TO SERVE
Add a julienne of smoked salmon and chopped chives.

Serves 8

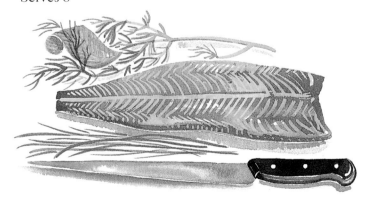

Cannelloni of Smoked Salmon and Quails' Eggs with a Chive Chantilly

From Mike Wamersley, chef, The Three Lions, Stuckton, Fordingbridge, Hants.

INGREDIENTS

8	quails' eggs, smoked or fresh
200ml (7fl.oz)	whipping cream
2 tbs	chopped chives
	lemon juice
	salt and pepper
4	slices smoked salmon
1	bunch rocket lettuce
25ml (1 fl.oz)	homemade vinaigrette
4 tbs	crisp croûtons

METHOD

If using fresh eggs boil eggs for 3 minutes and refresh in cold water. Peel carefully as they will still be runny inside.

Whip the cream until it almost forms ribbons but is still pouring. Season with chives and a squeeze of lemon juice and set chantilly aside.

Warm eggs in hot water, drain and season with salt and pepper. Smoked eggs will not require seasoning. Wrap 2 eggs per portion in smoked salmon to form a cannelloni shape tube.

Dress rocket with vinaigrette. Place cannelloni on a bed of croûtons and garnish with rocket. Serve with chive chantilly.

Serves 4

♀ *California Pinot Noir.*

SMOKED TROUT
AND CHAR

Smoked trout is often seen as a poor relation to smoked salmon which is a pity because good smoked trout is light and delicate with a beautiful deep pink flesh. As the taste is different from salmon, smoked trout can pair well with it and many other flavours. It makes an excellent salad with baby spinach. Make it into an unbaked cheesecake (no sugar) with cream cheese and soured cream, using unsweetened wholemeal biscuits as a base. Use it in fresh tomato soup, make it into chowder. What about hash with leftover potatoes and fried eggs?

Smoked char is similar to smoked trout but has a more delicate, clear flavour and an exquisitely beautiful, deep pink colour. It can be used in place of smoked trout. I have only found one regular supplier of smoked char, but it is worth the extra effort of ordering specially.

♟ *Auxerrois from Alsace; German Spatburgunder (Pinot Noir), dry Muller-Thurgau from Mosel Saar Ruwer, mature Riesling from the Pfalz; Tio Pepe sherry; California Gamay from Monterey; Australian Sauvignon Blanc; South African Gewurztraminer; Northern Highland single malt whisky.*

POTTED TROUT WRAPPED IN SMOKED SALMON

From Tony Bradley, Master Cook, Simpsons in the Strand, London

INGREDIENTS

250g (8 oz)	smoked trout, flaked
½	small onion, very finely chopped
	handful of chopped chives
150ml (¼ pt)	double cream
4	small slices smoked salmon
	fresh ground pepper
4	lemon wedges
4	sprigs dill
4	sprigs lollo rosso

METHOD

Mix smoked trout, onion and chives and blend together with cream. Season to taste.

Line 4 individual ramekins or other small moulds with slices of smoked salmon large enough to fold over the top, and fill with trout mixture. Chill several hours in the refrigerator.

Turn out on to a plate and garnish with lemon, dill and lollo rosso. There are several sauces that could accompany this if desired – dill mayonnaise, chive dressing – but it is not strictly necessary.

Serves 4

SMOKED FISH ROULADE

From Gillian Petty, Teviot Game Fare Smokery, Kelso,
Roxburghshire

INGREDIENTS

1	smoked trout
2 tsp	horseradish
250g (8 oz)	cream cheese
	salt and pepper
1	lemon, zest and juice
	dill, chives or flat parsley, chopped
500g (1 lb)	sliced smoked salmon
	lemon to garnish

METHOD

Skin and bone the trout. Flake the flesh and mix with horseradish, cream cheese, salt and pepper, zest and juice of lemon and chopped herbs.

Divide the trout mixture among the slices of smoked salmon, roll up around it and chill. Serve either in 5cm (2") lengths or sliced rounds.

Serves 8 as a starter

SMOKED EEL

Smoked eel, at its best, is a rival for smoked salmon. The flavour is rich, sweet and the texture is meaty and firm. Many northern Europeans – the Dutch, Germans, and Scandinavians – are as mad about smoked eel as we are about smoked salmon. For a special afternoon tea treat, serve smoked eel sandwiches with a fresh horseradish and chive butter spread on homemade soda bread. Serve with a pot of Lapsang Souchang.

♀ *Pinot Noir (chilled) or Auxerrois from Alsace; dry Muller-Thurgau from Mosel Saar Ruwer; Fino Pando sherry when eel is served plain; unoaked California Chardonnay; Pinot Noir or unoaked Chardonnay from Australia; South African Gewurztraminer; single malt from the Western Highlands.*

SALAD OF SMOKED EEL IN A SHALLOT DRESSING WITH PICKLED VEGETABLES AND HORSERADISH CREAM

From Paul Pavani, chef, Soho House, London

INGREDIENTS

PICKLED VEGETABLES

1.8 litres (3 pt)	white wine
2.4 litres (4 pt)	water
600ml (1 pt)	white wine vinegar
bouquet garni consisting of:	
1	bay leaf
1 tbs	pickling spices
6	juniper berries
	(all wrapped in muslin)
500g (1 lb)	sugar
	button onions

sliced red and green peppers
black olives
Italian capers
sliced gherkins

HORSERADISH CREAM

2 tbs	fresh grated horseradish
300 ml ($\frac{1}{2}$ pt)	double cream
	salt and pepper
juice of $\frac{1}{2}$	lemon
$\frac{1}{2}$ tbs	chopped dill

SHALLOT DRESSING

2 tbs	finely chopped shallots
2 tsp	chopped thyme
2 tsp	finely chopped garlic
	sprig of tarragon
1	bay leaf
25ml (1 fl.oz)	white wine vinegar
125ml (4 fl.oz)	olive oil
125g (4 oz)	baby spinach
$\frac{1}{4}$	curly endive (frisée)
$\frac{1}{4}$	oak leaf lettuce
500g (1 lb)	smoked eel fillets
	squeeze of lemon juice
	salt and pepper

METHOD

For pickled vegetables, bring all liquids to the boil
with the bouquet garni and sugar. Add onions and
simmer until tender. Remove and set aside. Repeat
with peppers. Combine in an airtight jar with olives,
capers and gherkins and allow to infuse for at
least 2 days. These will keep for 2 weeks when
refrigerated in an airtight container.

For horseradish cream, whisk all ingredients lightly to

a thick pouring consistency.

For shallot dressing, place all ingredients except oil in pan. The vinegar should just cover the shallots. Bring to a simmer and remove from heat. Allow to cool and whisk in oil a little at a time. Season with salt and pepper and fresh lemon juice to taste. To serve, dress the salad leaves with shallot dressing and add smoked eel and pickled vegetables to taste. Place in middle of a flat plate and pour some of the horseradish cream around the salad.

Serves 4

Smoked Eel with Baby Bok choy

INGREDIENTS

4	spring onions
1 tbs	sesame oil
3-4	heads baby bok choy, separated and sliced
1 tbs	Worcestershire sauce
250g (8 oz)	smoked eel fillets
1 tsp	pan toasted sesame seeds
	chopped chives, coriander or parsley
2	slices of lemon

CHEF'S TIP

Young, thin asparagus or baby leeks could also be used effectively if baby bok choy is not available.

METHOD

Preheat grill for 3-4 minutes.

Cut spring onions lengthways. Heat wok for 1 minute or until hot. Drizzle in sesame oil and allow oil to get hot. Add spring onions and stir fry until just starting to wilt. Add slices of baby bok choy and stir fry 15-30 seconds. Pour in Worcestershire sauce. Divide between two warmed plates.

Meanwhile, heat eel fillets under a very hot, preheated grill until just warm, about 1-2 minutes. Place on top of bok choy, garnish with sesame seeds and chopped chives. Drizzle over any of the sesame oil left in the wok. Cut lemon slice half way through, twist and place on one side.

Serves 2

♀ *Tio Pepe sherry.*

SMOKED TUNA

Smoked tuna is a very meaty fish and looks almost like raw beef. It is well suited to robust treatments, either Mediterranean or Oriental, so you can serve it with accompaniments for carpaccio or sashimi. Make it into a tartare with a raw egg and garlic or ginger. Use in a Salad Niçoise with smoked eggs.

♀ *Pinot Noir (chilled) or Auxerrois from Alsace; a mature Riesling from Germany; or Manzanilla Solear by Barbadillo.*

SMOKED TUNA, GARLIC AND LEMON GRASS KEBABS, WITH CORIANDER AND GINGER SAUCE

From Jonathan Fraser, chef, Bath Spa Hotel, Bath

INGREDIENTS

BUTTER SAUCE

500ml (18 fl.oz)	good homemade fish stock
½	glass white wine
½	glass Noilly Prat dry vermouth
2	diced shallots
100ml (3 ½ fl.oz)	double cream
250g (8 oz)	diced cold butter
6	large sticks of lemon grass
1kg (2 lb)	cold smoked tuna, cut into 2.5cm (1") cubes
1	whole head hot smoked garlic, peeled
2	red sweet peppers, cut into 2cm (1") pieces
1	courgette, sliced thin

| 1 | bunch coriander with stalks, chopped |
| 1 | finger-joint-sized piece of ginger, peeled and grated |

Prepare the sauce. To a pan add fish stock, white wine, dry vermouth and diced shallots. Reduce by ⅔. Add double cream and reduce again, at a slow simmer, by ⅓. Add cold diced butter and blend with hand mixer or whisk.

Prepare the kebabs using the lemon grass as a kebab stick. Alternate pieces of tuna, garlic, pepper and courgette.

Bake, grill or pan fry the kebabs for 15-20 minutes until cooked.

Set the sauce to a slow boil, infuse with the ginger and coriander and serve separately.

Serve with rice, baked sweet potatoes or polenta.

Serves 6

SMOKED HADDOCK

Smoked haddock is a very popular, traditional smoked fish. As smoking techniques have improved, good undyed smoked haddock now has a deep golden colour, which is much preferable to the dyed yellow variety. The taste is pronounced but not over-strong and the texture is quite firm. Many chefs like to cook with it because it harmonises so many different tastes. When you consider its versatility and low price, smoked haddock is very good value for money. It is, of course, the classic fish for kedgeree, which Hugh Forestier-Walker suggests additionally garnishing with smoked prawns.

♀ Auxerrois from Alsace; Fino Pando sherry; Fume Blanc from California; Australian Riesling; South African Chardonnay; or Speyside single malt whisky.

SMOKED HADDOCK BASQUAISE

From Carla Phillips, chef at Moorings, Wells next the Sea, Norfolk

INGREDIENTS

1.25kg (2 lb 12 oz)	smoked haddock
300ml (½ pt)	milk
300ml (½ pt)	water
3	large onions
750g (1 lb 10 oz)	tomatoes
	butter for frying
200g (7 oz)	green and black olives, stoned
3-4	cloves garlic, minced
	bay leaf, parsley, savoury, oregano
	pepper
50ml (2 fl.oz)	olive oil

Gently poach the haddock in equal quantities of milk and water, about 20 minutes. Peel and chop the onions. Peel, seed and chop the tomatoes. Melt butter and cook onions until transparent. Add tomatoes and cook 5 minutes. Add olives, garlic and herbs. Season to taste with fresh black pepper (the haddock already is salty).

Drain haddock and flake into tomato mixture. Add olive oil, mix well and continue to cook a few more minutes. Serve on hot plates.

Serves 4-6

♀ *Dos Cortados Oloroso sherry by Williams & Humbert; California Merlot.*

SMOKED HADDOCK FISH CAKES WITH AVOCADO SALAD

From Brian Baker, chef, The Abingdon, London

1kg (2 lb)	smoked haddock
600ml (1 pt)	milk
1	bay leaf
2	cloves garlic
	generous amount of chopped flat parsley

500g (1 lb)	dry mashed potato (no milk or butter)
	fine breadcrumbs
	oil, for frying

AVOCADO SALAD

1-2	avocados
juice of 1-2	lemons
250ml (8 fl.oz)	olive oil
	generous bunch of chervil
2 tbs	finely chopped shallots
	salt and pepper

METHOD

Skin the haddock and remove as many bones as possible. Poach the haddock in milk with a bay leaf for about 20 minutes but do not overcook. Remove from heat and allow to cool. Drain and flake. Mix with garlic, parsley and mashed potato but do not over mix. Season to taste, shape into 12 cakes and coat with breadcrumbs. Shallow fry in hot oil.

For the avocado salad, peel, stone and chop avocado into cubes. Mix with lemon juice, olive oil, chopped chervil, shallots, salt and pepper.

Scatter the salad over four or six dishes, place 2 or 3 fish cakes on each plate and garnish with chopped chervil.

Suggestion: serve with boiled new potatoes.

Serves 4-6

Y *Languedoc Blanc from France*

Smoked Haddock, Bubble and Squeak

From Gary Hollihead, chef, L'Escargot, London

½	primo cabbage, shredded
1	onion, peeled and sliced
	butter for sweating and frying
250g (8 oz)	mashed potato (without cream or butter)

SAUCE

600ml (1 pt)	vegetable stock
1	shallot
1	clove garlic
1	bunch tarragon
1 dsp	double cream
100g (4 oz)	unsalted butter chilled and diced
1	lemon
	dry white vermouth or dry white wine
1	bunch chives
300g (10 oz)	smoked haddock fillet
2	eggs, poached

Blanch cabbage in boiling, salted water. Refresh in cold water. Sweat the sliced onion in butter in a covered pan without colouring. Mix mashed potato with cooked cabbage and onion and form into neatly shaped potato cakes. Shallow fry in butter for 6-7 minutes, until golden on both sides.

To make the sauce, reduce the vegetable stock with chopped shallot, a clove of garlic and the tarragon stalks. Strain and add the cream. Whisk in about 25-

50g (1-2 oz) cold diced butter. Finish with a few
drops of lemon juice and a splash of dry white
vermouth or dry white wine. Strain and add chopped
chives and tarragon leaves.

Fry the smoked haddock in a non-stick pan until
golden on both sides. Place the potato cakes on the
plate, lay the haddock on top. Reheat the poached
eggs and place on top. Dribble the sauce around the
plate, give a turn of black pepper.

TO SERVE
Deep-fried crisps of carrot and parsnip are the
recommended vegetables with this dish, along with
roasted shallots.

Serves 2

SMOKED HADDOCK PUFFS

*Supplied by Neil Goldie, chef, London Catering Service. Taken from a
Victorian manuscript recipe.*

INGREDIENTS	
500g (1 lb)	cooked, boned smoked haddock (or cod)
50g (2 oz)	self raising flour
2	eggs, beaten
¼ tsp	cayenne pepper
3-4 tbs	of the liquor the fish was cooked in
	oil for deep frying

METHOD
Flake the fish and mix with the flour and beaten eggs, then add the cayenne pepper and enough of the fish liquor to make the mixture the consistency of a

smooth choux paste. Heat the oil but do not let it
smoke, and drop in a tablespoonful at a time, cooking
until they puff up and are a golden brown all over.

Makes 30-40 pieces

♀ *Dos Cortados Oloroso sherry by Williams & Humbert.*

SMOKED HADDOCK AND FENNEL SALAD

From Peter Dodd, chef, Wig & Mitre, Lincoln

INGREDIENTS

500g (1lb)	smoked haddock fillet
	salt and pepper
juice of 2	lemons
4 tbs	extra virgin olive oil
	chopped chives
2	medium bulbs fennel
	mixed salad leaves

METHOD

Slice the haddock as thinly as you would smoked
salmon. Lay it on a tray and season with salt, pepper,
lemon juice, olive oil and chopped chives. Allow to
marinate 10 minutes.

Cover a large serving plate with the thin slices of
marinated haddock and cover with fine slices of
fennel and mixed salad leaves.
Use the
marinade as a
salad dressing.

Serves 4 as starter,
2 as light main

SMOKED COD

Smoked cod takes well to a whole range of treatments and is especially suited to baking as it is a thick fillet. Make it à la Portuguese, on a bed of onion, potato and tomato with a bit of garlic and fresh herbs. Roast it under a tent of smoked salmon or smoked trout skin.

Smoked cod's roe is the ideal ingredient for homemade taramasalata and its deep colour means no added dye is necessary for it to look appealing.

♟ *Fino Pando sherry; Auxerrois from Alsace; California Fume*

SMOKED COD AND SPINACH SOUFFLE

From Debbie Howard, Shetland Smokehouse, Skeld, Shetland

INGREDIENTS	
750g (1½ lb)	fresh spinach
1	medium onion, chopped
1 tbs	olive oil
3 tsp	butter
4 tsp	flour
250ml (8 fl.oz)	milk
	pinch of cayenne pepper and fresh ground nutmeg

6	egg yolks
3 tsp	grated Parmesan cheese
	salt and fresh black pepper
500g (1 lb)	smoked cod
7	egg whites
	pinch of cream of tartar

METHOD

Wash and trim the spinach. Cook without water until wilted and tender. Drain thoroughly, chop very fine and drain again, pressing out any liquid. Sauté onion in olive oil until translucent, stir in chopped spinach.

Melt butter in heavy pan and stir in flour. Cook roux 3-4 minutes without colouring and then whisk in cold milk. Cook over low heat until thickened, season with cayenne and nutmeg. Remove from heat and beat in egg yolks one at a time. Add Parmesan cheese. Return to low heat and stir a few minutes. Remove from heat, add spinach mixture and season with salt and pepper to taste.

Steam smoked cod for 12 minutes. Cool and flake. Add to spinach mixture. Whisk egg whites with cream of tartar until they form stiff peaks. Stir ¼ of the whites into the spinach mixture, then carefully fold in the rest. Pour into a buttered soufflé dish and bake in an oven preheated to 180°C, 350°F, Gas Mark 4 for 35-40 minutes. Serve immediately.

Serves 4 as a starter

KIPPERS

Kippers have a pronounced taste that people either love or hate. They're wonderful for a leisurely breakfast treat and can be either grilled, fried or poached for 4-5 minutes, or baked in foil for about 15 minutes. Seasoning with lemon juice takes away some of the strong smell.

♀ *Kippers at breakfast are meant for strong tea like English Breakfast, Earl Grey or Darjeeling. They eluded all matching with wine, but do go well with beer; either a good lager or a pale ale. They also go especially well with single malt whisky from the Western Highlands.*

KIPPER FILLETS WRAPPED IN BACON WITH MUSTARD AND AVOCADO VINAIGRETTE

From Debbie Howard, Shetland Smokehouse, Skeld, Shetland

INGREDIENTS

8	rashers unsmoked back bacon
8	kipper fillets
	olive oil for baking tray
1	medium avocado
juice of ½	lemon
2 tbs	olive oil
2	cloves garlic, crushed
2 tsp	minced onion
2 tsp	white wine vinegar
½ tsp	sugar
	pepper

METHOD

Wrap bacon around kipper fillets. Put on oiled tray and grill for 15 minutes.

Meanwhile prepare avocado vinaigrette. Cut, peel and stone avocado. Add lemon juice and mash flesh with a wooden spoon or in a food processor. Whisk in olive oil, then add remaining ingredients. Stir well. Cover bottom of plates with vinaigrette, place warmed kipper fillet on top. Serve with boiled new potatoes.

Serves 8 as a starter, 4 as a main course

SMOKED MACKEREL

Smoked mackerel is very widely available as fillets and is often coated in various cracked peppers, or even with chillies. Plain fillets are good with a horseradish and apple cream sauce.

It makes a good, strongly flavoured pâté which goes well on rye or sourdough bread. Debbie Howard of the Shetland Smokehouse suggests making devilled eggs with a soured cream and smoked mackerel dressing added to the yolks.

♀ *Languedoc Blanc from France; Manzanilla Solear by Barbadillo or Tio Pepe sherries; a good German Riesling; and California Fume Blanc.*

SMOKED FISH SALAD

From Mark Holmes, Scotts Restaurant & Oyster Bar, London

INGREDIENTS	
125g (4 oz)	smoked mackerel
125g (4 oz)	smoked eel
125g (4 oz)	smoked trout
125g (4 oz)	smoked salmon
125g (4 oz)	smoked cod's roe
2	shallots, finely chopped
1heaped tsp	Dijon mustard
2 tsp	caster sugar
2	lemons, juice and zest
600ml (1 pt)	extra virgin olive oil
	salt and pepper
	mixed lettuce leaves:
	lollo rosso, oak leaf, radiccio, curly endive
2	free range eggs
	pinch of celery salt
1	bunch finely chopped chives

Flake all the fish gently by hand and mix, add shallots and set aside.

Mix mustard, sugar and lemon zest into the lemon juice then slowly whisk in the olive oil. Season to taste and set aside.

Wash lettuce and tear by hand into bite size pieces.

Boil eggs for 3 ½ minutes then refresh under cold water. When cold, peel and set aside.

Just before serving, toss the lettuce in a large bowl with the dressing then place on four plates, almost covering them. Scatter the fish and shallot mixture over the lettuce.

Top each plate with half a boiled egg, being careful not to spill the yolk which should still be a bit soft. Sprinkle a little celery salt on the eggs and a handful of chives over the whole salad.

Serves 4 as a main course

"KEDGEREE" OF SMOKED MACKEREL

From Stephen Barrett, wine and food writer

I N G R E D I E N T S

2	large onions
1 tbs	butter
4 tbs	mild curry paste
½ tsp	turmeric
250g (8 oz)	cooked short-grained brown rice
4	smoked mackerel
4	eggs
1 litre (1 ¾ pt)	milk
4	hard boiled eggs
4	sprigs fresh coriander

Coarsely chop onions and sauté in butter.
Mix together the curry paste and turmeric
and cook for 2 minutes. Add cooked rice
and mix together. Remove skins and
bones from smoked mackerel. Break
into large chunks and add to the rice.
Cook 2 minutes.

Mix raw eggs and milk, add to the
rice and stir continually for 2-3
minutes over high heat until
bound together. Serve with
sliced hard boiled egg
and garnish with
coriander sprigs.

Serves 4

SMOKED FISH SOUP WITH CROUTONS AND ROUILLE

From Chris Suter, Bishopstrow House, Warminster, Wilts.

INGREDIENTS

75g (3 oz)	smoked mackerel
75g (3 oz)	smoked haddock
75g (3 oz)	red mullet
75g (3 oz)	hake
75g (3 oz)	bass
1.2 litres (2 pt)	fish stock made from bones including smoked fish bones and skin
1	onion chopped
2 tbs	olive oil
1	large clove garlic, finely chopped
1	potato, chopped
½	glass white wine
2	plum tomatoes, skinned, seeded and chopped
	salt and pepper
	thyme, tarragon, fennel green or flat parsley, chopped

METHOD

Remove all skin and bones from the fish and use in making stock. Cut fish into 2cm (½") cubes.

Fry onion in olive oil until softened and add garlic. Cook a few minutes more, add potato and continue to cook. Add white wine to deglaze, then add fish stock. Stir well and add diced fish. Cook for 10 minutes over gentle heat. Season to taste, add tomato and herbs.

Serve with homemade rouille and croûtons and some good, grated smoked cheese.

Serves 6

♀ *California Fume Blanc.*

SMOKED OYSTERS

Smoked oysters are often derided as a terrible way of treating an ingredient that is so good fresh, but then most people have only tasted smoked oysters out of a tin. Freshly smoked ones are a different matter entirely. Chris Fisher, chef of the Edgwarebury Hotel in Elstree suggests serving them as smoked angels on horseback, wrapped in blanched streaky bacon. Use them in a beef and oyster pie. Or use them in place of oysters in an oriental oyster sauce.

♀ *Anjou Blanc or Languedoc Blanc from France; Tio Pepe sherry; California late harvest Riesling.*

PASTA WITH SMOKED OYSTERS AND GORGONZOLA

From Jamieson Clark, chef, Ciao Baby Cucina, Washington, D.C. - appeared in Nation's Restaurant News

INGREDIENTS	
350g (12 oz)	pasta bow ties, farfalle or other similar shape
2 tbs	olive oil
	handful fresh sage, chopped
2	cloves garlic, minced
½	glass white wine
250g (8 oz)	smoked oysters
50ml (2 fl.oz)	double cream
	fresh milled pepper
125g (4 oz)	Gorgonzola cheese, crumbled
	chopped flat leaf parsley
25g (1 oz)	pine nuts, toasted

Bring a large pot of salted water to the boil and cook the pasta according to package directions, about 10 minutes. It should still be *al dente*.

Meanwhile, heat the olive oil with half the chopped sage over a low flame, 3-5 minutes to flavour the oil. Remove the sage and add the chopped garlic to the oil. Cook slowly a further 3 minutes. Add the white wine and reduce by half. Add the smoked oysters and the cream and stir. Give a couple of gratings of fresh pepper. Just before serving toss with the crumbled Gorgonzola. Garnish each dish with chopped parsley, sage and toasted pine nuts.

Serves 4

SMOKED MUSSELS

Smoked mussels are wonderfully juicy, briny and quite a lusty taste; a seafood-lovers' seafood. Their larger size makes green-lipped mussels from New Zealand especially well suited for smoking. Minola produces these and they serve them with a dipping sauce of soy, runny honey like acacia and chopped garlic; ginger would also be good.

♀ *Pinot Noir (chilled) from Alsace; Oloroso Seco sherry by Barbadillo; dry Grauburgunder (Pinot Gris) from Nahe, Rheingau or Rheinhessen in Germany; California late harvest Riesling; South African Chenin Blanc; and Islay single malt whisky.*

PASTRY PUFF OF SMOKED MUSSELS WITH CUMIN

From Chris Fisher, chef, Edgwarebury Hotel, Elstree, Herts.

INGREDIENTS	
125g (4 oz)	clarified butter
125g (4 oz)	chopped onions
1	clove garlic, finely minced
1 tsp	cumin
150ml (¼ pt)	white wine
150ml (¼ pt)	fish stock
75ml (3 fl.oz)	double cream
125g (4 oz)	puff pastry
500g (1 lb)	washed and chopped large leaf spinach
	nutmeg
	salt and pepper
16	hot-smoked New Zealand green – lipped mussels
75g (3 oz)	cold butter, cubed

In a hot pan and in half the clarified butter, sweat half the onions and all the garlic, covered so that it does not colour. Add cumin, stir and add wine. Reduce and add fish stock. Reduce, add double cream and pass through a sieve. Keep warm till needed.

Meanwhile, roll out the puff pastry and cut into four 7.5cm (3") discs. Bake for 5-7 minutes in an oven preheated to 180°C, 350°F, Gas Mark 4 and allow to cool. With the point of a sharp knife inserted between the layers, gently prise each apart into two discs.

Pan fry the spinach and remaining onion in remaining clarified butter for less than a minute, adding grated nutmeg, salt and fresh ground pepper to taste.

Heat the mussels under a grill which has been brushed with a little butter.

Carefully spoon the spinach on to the bottom discs, arrange four mussels on top "falling" from each puff.

Finish sauce by whisking in cold cubed butter. Pour a small amount over the mussels and the rest around the puffs. Place lid askew on top and serve.

Serves 4

♀ *Cotes du Rhone from France.*

SMOKED SCALLOPS

Smoked scallops are really sinfully good, the sort of taste you'd try to invent. The combination of sweet and smoky tastes combined with a succulent texture is incredible. Jonathan Cooksley of the Valley Smoke House serves them with a lemon and ginger dressing. They can also be served warmed, as you would for fresh scallops. Try them with basil or coriander-infused olive oil on a bed of finely puréed cooked carrot. As good as queen scallops are, the larger smoked king scallops are really worth searching for.

♀ *Gewurztraminer from Alsace; Fino Pando sherry; California late harvest Riesling.*

SMOKED SCALLOP, SAFFRONED FENNEL AND TOMATO SALAD WITH CURRIED VINAIGRETTE

From Jerome Dutois, Head Chef, Harrods, London

INGREDIENTS

2	beefsteak tomatoes, peeled
12	smoked scallops
40g (1½ oz)	chopped shallots
	small bunch chives, finely chopped
1 tsp	Worcestershire sauce
40 ml (1½ fl.oz)	homemade vinaigrette with
½ tsp	prepared curry powder
	salt and pepper
100g (3½ oz)	mâche lettuce (lamb's)
125g (4 oz)	sliced fennel, marinated overnight in olive oil, saffron and lemon juice
	poppy seeds
4	sprigs chervil

Cut two large slices from each of the peeled tomatoes. Remove seeds from the remaining tomato and dice finely.

Mix the scallops with the diced tomato, shallots, finely chopped chives, Worcestershire sauce and ¼ of the curry vinaigrette. Check seasoning and add salt and pepper if necessary.

Place the cleaned mâche lettuce in the centre of 4 dinner plates. Lay three slices of saffroned fennel on top. Place three scallops in the centre of the salad and lay the sliced tomato on top.

Sprinkle curry vinaigrette around the plate. Decorate with poppy seeds and chervil.

Serves 4

SMOKED QUAILS' EGGS

Smoked quails' eggs are extremely useful as a garnish, especially when you consider that they come already peeled. Use them for particularly delicate devilled egg canapes, topped with caviar.
Smoked hens' eggs will have the same smoky flavour.

SMOKED QUAILS' EGGS WITH SMOKED HADDOCK AND CHEESE SAUCE

From Tony Bradley, Master Cook, Simpsons in the Strand, London

INGREDIENTS

250g (8 oz)	smoked haddock
600ml (1 pt)	milk
600ml (1 pt)	double cream
12	smoked quails' eggs
50g (2 oz)	grated cheddar cheese
25g (1 oz)	grated Parmesan cheese
	cayenne pepper

METHOD

Cook the smoked haddock in milk and flake the fish. Put aside. Add cream to the milk and reduce slowly, at a gentle simmer, until it coats the back of a spoon. Season to taste with salt if necessary.

Arrange the fish in individual, heatproof dishes. Put the whole quails' eggs on top, three to a portion. Pour the cream sauce over the top. Add the grated cheeses and sprinkle a bit of cayenne pepper on top. Grill until golden brown.

Serves 4

♀ *Auxerrois from Alsace.*

Scotch Quails' Eggs

From Chris Fisher, chef, Edgwarebury Hotel, Elstree, Herts.

INGREDIENTS

175g (6 oz)	smoked haddock
1	egg, separated
200ml (7 fl. oz)	double cream, chilled
	cayenne pepper
	handful of fresh parsley
	handful of fresh mint
200-250g (7-8 oz)	fresh breadcrumbs
	salt and white pepper
24	smoked quails' eggs
	oil for deep frying

INGREDIENTS

Process smoked haddock with 1 egg white.

Force through a fine sieve. Carefully incorporate the chilled cream in a bowl over ice. Season with salt and cayenne pepper. To test the mixture, wrap a spoonful in clingfilm and poach in almost simmering water. Check consistency and seasoning. Refrigerate mousse for at least an hour.

Finely chop the parsley and mint, add to the fresh breadcrumbs and season with white pepper. Roll each quail egg in the smoked haddock mousse and roll quickly in breadcrumbs. Refrigerate again before deep frying in hot oil until golden. Serve as quickly as possible.

Makes 24

♀ *Tio Pepe sherry.*

SMOKED CHICKEN AND SMOKED TURKEY

Smoked chicken and smoked turkey are the answer to sandwich boredom. Spread some good bread with a bit of chutney – mango, tomato and ginger, onion and coriander, walnut – or cranberry sauce – and add a bit of green. Jonathan Cooksley of The Valley Smoke House does endless variations of smoked chicken soup, using the whole carcass for the stock; try it with red pepper, sweetcorn, or parsnip. Serve either chicken or turkey as a warm salad with chick peas, or with avocado and soured cream, or as part of a Russian salad with diced potato, carrot and peas.

♀ *Languedoc Blanc from France; Manzanilla Solear sherry by Barbadillo; German Spatburgunder or mature Riesling from the Pfalz; Australian Pinot Noir; South African Chardonnay.*

LINGUINI WITH SMOKED CHICKEN AND ARTICHOKES

From Brian Baker, chef, The Abingdon, London

INGREDIENTS	
1	whole smoked chicken
2	small tins baby artichokes
1	sprig thyme
1	sprig sage
1	sprig parsley
4	cloves garlic
2-4	dried chillies
300ml (½ pt)	olive oil
2x500g (1lb)	packets linguini

Remove meat from the chicken carcass, discarding the fat and skin. Shred meat into small pieces.

Drain the artichokes, rinse, drain again and cut into quarters.

Destalk herbs and chop leaves finely.

Put the garlic, chillies and a small amount of olive oil into a blender and blend until smooth. Then add the remaining olive oil and store in a large jar.

Cook the linguini in abundant boiling, salted water with a bit of oil in it to keep the pasta from sticking.

Meanwhile, put a ladle of the garlic and chilli oil in a pan and add the quarters of artichokes, smoked chicken and herbs and heat.

Drain the linguini, saving a cupful of the cooking water in case the pasta needs a bit of moistening. Toss the artichoke and chicken mixture with the linguini, reserving a bit of chicken and artichoke to put on top of each portion. Season to taste. Serve with fresh grated Parmesan cheese.

Serves 8

♀ *Cotes du Rhone from France.*

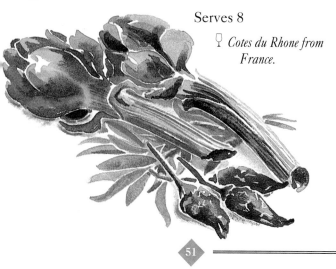

SMOKED DUCK

Smoked duck is a favourite with everyone who tastes it. Something about the fattiness of the meat really suits smoked flavour. Like chicken and turkey, smoked duck would make a wonderful sandwich or salad. Pears poached in white or red wine with mulled wine spices go well with smoked duck.

♀ *Auxerrois from France; Dos Cortados Oloroso sherry by Williams & Humbert; Rheinhessen Portuguieser or mature Riesling from the Pfalz; California Pinot Noir or Cabernet Sauvignon; South African Pinot Noir; single malt from the Northern or Western Highlands.*

CHARTREUSE OF SMOKED DUCK BREAST WITH BLACKCURRANTS ON A HONEY AND MUSTARD SEED DRESSING

From Ian Webb, head chef, Foley Lodge Hotel, Stockcross, Berks.

INGREDIENTS

300g (10oz)	smoked duck breast, thinly sliced into strips
250g (8 oz)	blackcurrants
4 tsp	double cream
2 tsp	Créme de Cassis

DRESSING
150ml (¼ pt)	sunflower oil
75ml (3 fl.oz)	white wine vinegar
	juice of 1 lime
2 tsp	wholegrain mustard
2 tsp	mustard seeds
75g (3 oz)	clear honey

125g (4 oz)   leek cut into fine julienne
               and deep fried
4   sprigs fresh chervil

METHOD

Line 4 timbales or small cups with thinly sliced duck
breast, skin side up so that when it is turned out a
striped effect is achieved.

In a mixing bowl combine the blackcurrants with the
cream and Créme de Cassis.

Half fill the timbales with the blackcurrant mixture,
then press in a layer of smoked duck breast and fill to
the top of the timbale with more blackcurrant
mixture.

Turn over the ends of the smoked duck slices (a small
piece may be needed in the centre) to seal in the
blackcurrants. Refrigerate to set for at least 1 hour.

For the dressing: mix all ingredients well until
combined. (A food processor is ideal for this.) Add salt
if necessary.

TO SERVE
Take the chartreuses carefully from the timbales and
place in the centre of 4 plates. Drizzle the dressing
around the chartreuse, top with deep-fried leek and
garnish with freshly picked chervil.

Serves 4

♀ *French Cabernet Sauvignon.*

SMOKED DUCK SALAD

From Chris Suter, chef, Bishopstrow House, Warminster, Wilts.

INGREDIENTS

1	smoked duck breast
50 ml (2 fl.oz)	walnut oil
50g (2 oz)	oyster mushrooms, chopped
25g (1 oz)	walnuts, roughly chopped
25g (1 oz)	hazelnuts, roughly chopped
25g (1 oz)	almonds
25g (1 oz)	raisins
50g (2 oz)	dried apricots
25g (1 oz)	dates
50 ml (2 fl.oz)	blackcurrant vinegar

assorted salad leaves – rocket, mâche, lollo rosso

VINAIGRETTE

100ml (3½ fl.oz)	walnut oil
80ml (3 fl.oz)	peanut oil
50ml (2 fl.oz)	white wine vinegar
	salt and pepper to taste
	herbs to garnish
15g (½oz)	toasted sesame seeds

METHOD

Slice breast thinly, toss in a hot pan with walnut oil and oyster mushrooms for 2-3 minutes. Add all dried nuts and fruit except sesame seeds. Allow to cook for 1 minute then deglaze the pan with the blackcurrant vinegar and season to taste. Dress the salad leaves with the vinaigrette, place neatly on plate. Arrange the hot duck slices, mushrooms, nuts and fruit carefully. Spoon over any pan juices and garnish with herbs. Sprinkle with sesame seeds.

Serves 4

♀ *Dos Cortados Oloroso sherry by Williams & Humbert.*

Smoked Guinea Fowl, Pheasant and Quail

These birds are all slightly gamey and moister than smoked chicken. Because they're rich tasting, they combine interestingly with full flavours. Try a warm salad of cold smoked quail tossed in a wok with a bit of walnut oil and pine nuts.

♀ Auxerrois or Gewurztraminer from Alsace; German Auslese Riesling; California late harvest Riesling; Australian Pinot Noir.

Smoked Pheasant Paté

From, Neil Goldie, executive chef, London Catering Service

INGREDIENTS

1	smoked pheasant
250g (8 oz)	veal
750g (1½ lb)	smoked streaky bacon
3	eggs
150ml (¼ pt)	whisky
	handful of fresh parsley
1 tbs	fresh thyme
1 tsp	each juniper berries and coriander seeds
	salt, pepper and nutmeg

METHOD

Bone the pheasant carefully, reserving the best pieces whole. Mince the scraps with the veal and just over ⅔ of the bacon, leaving enough to line the dish. Beat the eggs and whisky and mix these into the forcemeat, with chopped herbs, crushed spices, salt, pepper and nutmeg. Leave in a cool place for a few hours for the flavours to mature. Then line a large terrine with strips of bacon and build up layers of alternate forcemeat and pieces of pheasant, ending with forcemeat. Cover with more strips of bacon, then foil, then a lid. Stand dish in a pan of water and bake for 2½ hours at 150°C, 300°F, Gas Mark 2. Cool under a light weight and serve the next day.

Serves 10-12

ROAST SMOKED GUINEA FOWL WITH MUSHY PEAS AND A SAUCE OF OLD MADEIRA

From Adam Saville, chef, Cricklade Hotel & Country Club, Cricklade, Wilts.

INGREDIENTS	
125g (4 oz)	dried marrowfat peas
½ tsp	bicarbonate of soda
2 tbs	wine vinegar
2 x 1kg (2lb)	smoked guinea fowl
	olive oil
	unsalted butter
14	shallots
1 tsp	sugar

SAUCE

	bones from guinea fowl
	olive oil
	unsalted butter
100ml (3 ½ fl.oz)	red wine vinegar
150ml (¼ pt)	dry Madeira
300ml (½ pt)	homemade brown chicken stock
	sprig fresh rosemary

GARNISH

75g (3 oz)	fresh peas
12	baby carrots
2 tsp	unsalted butter

METHOD

Soak marrowfat peas and bicarbonate of soda in plenty of water for 24 hours. Rinse well, cover with fresh water, bring to boil and simmer for 45 minutes until soft. Season with vinegar, salt and pepper. Keep warm.

Remove legs and breasts from each bird. Heat oil and butter in heavy pan, fry legs for 1 minute on each side and breasts for 30 seconds. Season and place in preheated oven at 170°C, 350°F, Gas Mark 4 with carcasses for 10 minutes.

Poach 12 shallots in boiling water with sugar for 5 minutes, drain and refresh. Fry in a little oil and butter and place in the oven with the guinea fowl for 15 minutes. Remove from oven, leave to rest for 10 minutes. Keep warm, covered in foil.

Chop the carcasses in small pieces. In a heavy pan, heat oil and butter and fry the carcasses and two chopped shallots. Sweat until the shallots are soft and remove excess fat. Add red wine vinegar and reduce until completely evaporated. Add the Madeira, reduce by half, add chicken stock and rosemary, reduce by half or until it coats a spoon. Pass through a fine sieve and season with salt and pepper.

Boil fresh peas and carrots for 1 minute in salted water, drain and toss in a little butter.

Place mushy peas in centre of plates with guinea fowl breasts and legs on top. Arrange roast shallots, peas and baby carrots around guinea fowl and spoon sauce over and around.

Serves 4

SMOKED PORK

Smoked pork comes in any number of different cuts. Smoked bacon is the most familiar and is suitable for any recipe that calls for bacon. It is especially suited to a salad of bitter greens – spinach, escarole, frisée, endive, dandelion greens - with croûtons and warm lardons of bacon. Soak Agen prunes in brandy, wrap in smoked bacon and cook for especially good devils on horseback.

♀ *Pinot Noir (chilled) from Alsace; German Spatburgunder (Pinot Noir).*

TERRINE OF SMOKED COLLAR, HOCK AND GAMMON

From Chris Fisher, chef, Edgwarebury Hotel, Elstree, Herts.

INGREDIENTS

3kg (6-7 lb)	fatty, smoked collar, hock and gammon
2.5k (5 lb)	ham or veal bones
2	pigs' trotters
6	large onions
1	head celery
75g (3 oz)	clarified butter
600ml (1 pt)	white wine
	fresh pepper
2 tsp	rubbed thyme
¼ tsp	mixed spice

METHOD

Cut meats into 5cm (2") cubes. Blanch, drain and rinse all bones and meat, including trotters.

In a large pot cover bones and meat with cold water.

Add two quartered onions and head of celery with heart removed. Bring to a boil and simmer for about 4 hours, until slightly overcooked. Skim continuously.

Remove meat from pan and reserve. Strain juices through muslin and leave to set in refrigerator. Remove any fat from the surface.

While still warm, pick the backfat from the meat and render by cooking in boiling water until all the fat is released; boil off the rest of the water. Pick the meat from the bones and keep in pieces as large as possible.

Peel and slice the remaining onions, sauté slowly in clarified butter until golden. Add white wine and allow to cook down. Add thyme, pepper and mixed spice. Add to picked meat.

Line a terrine with cling film and pack the meat and onion mix into this, ensuring that all picked meat is lengthwise in the terrine. Add cooking juice up to the top. Cover, press with a weight and refrigerate for at least 3 hours or overnight.

When set, pour a 5mm ($\frac{1}{8}$") layer of the rendered fat over the surface. Allow to set in the refrigerator for another 2-3 hours. Remove from terrine mould.

Serve with chutney or picalilli.

Serves 10-12

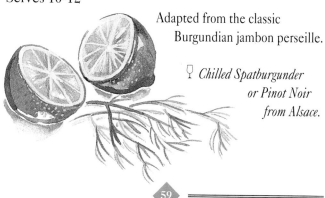

Adapted from the classic
Burgundian jambon perseille.

♀ *Chilled Spatburgunder
or Pinot Noir
from Alsace.*

SMOKED VENISON

Smoked venison is very lean, has a mild game taste and a deep colour. It's become quite a darling of chefs. Try wrapping slices around asparagus spears, or smoked venison mixed with cream and herbs piped into baked choux puffs. It's good with avocado, and with black olives and tomato. Whole, smoked venison roast has a more intensified flavour of venison.

♀ Auxerrois from Alsace, Cotes du Rhone; Oloroso Seco sherry by Barbadillo; Rheinhessen Portuguieser or a mature Riesling from Germany; California Zinfandel; Australian Cabernet Sauvignon; Speyside or Western Highland single malt.

RAMEKIN OF SMOKED VENISON AND PIGEON

From Frances Atkins, chef, Shaw's, London

INGREDIENTS

250g (8 oz)	smoked venison
1	pigeon
½	small diced green pepper
100g (4 oz)	chicken livers
1	egg
1 dsp	brandy
300ml (12 fl.oz)	double cream
	fresh ground pepper
1	clove garlic, crushed

METHOD

Line the ramekin dish with smoked venison leaving an overlap to make the lid. Remove breasts from the pigeon and cut into small dice and mix with the green pepper.

Blend chicken livers, egg, brandy and cream in a food processor. Season with pepper and garlic. Add pigeon mixture and spoon into lined ramekin. Cover with the overlapping venison.

Cover with aluminium foil. Place ramekin in *bain marie* and bake at 200°C, 400°F, Gas Mark 6 for 30 minutes until firm to the touch.

Turn out from ramekin and serve with soft fruits, such as raspberries.

Serves 4 as a starter

HOT–SMOKED VENISON ROAST WITH FRUIT COMPOTE

From Neil Goldie, executive chef, London Catering Service

INGREDIENTS

FRUIT COMPOTE

2	eating apples, peeled and thinly sliced
8	pitted prunes, pre-soaked
8	dried apricots, pre-soaked
1	large pear, peeled and thinly sliced
2 tsp	wine vinegar
	cinnamon stick
25g (1 oz)	brown sugar
	cloves
1	haunch of hot-smoked venison or boneless haunch, rolled
1 tbs	crushed juniper berries
1 tsp	grated lemon rind
	grated nutmeg
	fresh ground black pepper
	olive oil

Prepare fruit compote, best done the day before. Combine all ingredients and simmer over low heat for ½ hour, stirring occasionally. Remove from heat, take out cloves and cinnamon stick and set aside to cool.

Preheat oven to 190°C, 375°F, Gas Mark 5.

Prepare the roast. Place joint of meat on large square of aluminium foil. Sprinkle with juniper berries, lemon rind and nutmeg. Season with pepper only - no salt. Drizzle with olive oil and wrap into loose parcel.

Roast for 1-1½ hours. The meat should be pink in the middle, like roast beef. When ready to serve, slice thinly on to a very hot serving dish. Heat fruit compote and serve separately.

Serve with roast potatoes, red cabbage and a selection of root vegetables.

Serves 6-8

PATTIES OF COLD SMOKED VENISON WITH CITRUS SAUCE

From Nichola Fletcher, Fletcher's Fine Foods, Auchtermuchty

INGREDIENTS

175g (6 oz)	pre-sliced cold-smoked venison
2	shallots
1	orange
2	lemons
2 tbs	olive or walnut oil
	freshly ground black pepper
	mixed salad leaves

Dice the smoked venison and the shallots into tiny pieces. Squeeze the juice from the orange and lemons into a small jug and whisk in the oil and black pepper. Stir half of this into the chopped venison and shallots.

Arrange salad leaves on to four plates, leaving a well in the centre. Place an oiled circular pastry cutter in the well and pack 1/4 of the smoked venison/shallot mixture firmly into the cutter. Lift the cutter off carefully and repeat on each plate. Drizzle remaining dressing over the salad leaves.

Serves 4 as starter

MIXED SALAD WITH SMOKED VENISON STRIPS

From Nichola Fletcher, Fletcher's Fine Foods, Auchtermuchty

INGREDIENTS

175g (6 oz)	smoked venison
125g (4 oz)	feta cheese
125g (4 oz)	sunflower seeds or walnuts
2	cloves garlic, minced
2 tsp	Dijon mustard
	salt and pepper to taste
1 tbs	balsamic vinegar
3 tbs	good olive oil
	mixed salad leaves or edible flowers

METHOD

Cut the smoked venison into strips. Cut the feta cheese into small cubes. Fry the sunflower seeds or walnuts until golden and crisp. Mix the garlic, mustard, salt and pepper into the balsamic vinegar and whisk in the oil. Toss all ingredients together just before serving.

Serves 4 as a starter or light lunch

"TAGLIATELLE" OF SMOKED VENISON WITH HORSERADISH

From Nichola Fletcher, Fletcher's Fine Foods, Auchtermuchty

INGREDIENTS

1 tbs	finely grated horseradish
1 heaped tbs	crème fraîche
1 tsp	Dijon mustard
1 tsp	fine brown sugar
175g (6 oz)	pre-sliced hot-smoked venison
2	large beetroots, freshly cooked but still *al dente*

CHEF'S TIP

To serve as a main course, double the quantities given and serve with a generous helping of good mashed potato. Good prepared horseradish cream can be used instead of the fresh horseradish.

METHOD

Mix the horseradish, crème fraîche, mustard and sugar to taste. Slice (or cut with scissors) the smoked venison slices into long strips about 1cm (1/2") thick and gently fold into the creamed horseradish. Slice the beetroots into either matchsticks or rounds. Arrange them in a circle or nest and pile a little heap of the horseradish and venison "tagliatelle" into the centre. Avoid combining the beetroot and the venison too soon or the beetroot will bleed into the pale sauce.

Serves 4 as starter

SMOKED MUTTON AND MACON

Smoked mutton is something that once tasted will never be forgotten. It tastes very strongly of lamb, the flavour is very deep and the texture is very meaty. For a cold winter day this is the ideal Sunday roast. Again, it also is very good for sandwiches – on sourdough bread – or in salads. Try it in a warm salad with a hot orange marmalade dressing made spicy with a bit of chilli oil.

Smoked macon is mutton ham that has first been brined, then air-dried before smoking and aging, much like Parma ham. Roll slices of macon around poached kumquats – the sweet tanginess cuts through the muttony richness.

♀ *French Cabernet Sauvignon; Tio Pepe sherry; German Spatlese Riesling; California Gamay or late harvest Riesling; South African Gewurztraminer or Cabernet Sauvignon; Islay single malt whisky.*

CABBAGE AND SMOKED MUTTON

From Neil Goldie, executive chef, London Catering Service

INGREDIENTS

3	medium savoy cabbages
1kg (2 lb)	smoked mutton
	salt, pepper, ground cloves
½ tsp	allspice
900ml (1½ pt)	veal stock

METHOD

Cut the cabbages in half and boil in salted water for 15 minutes. Drain and refresh in cold water. Drain well. Line the bottom of a fireproof dish with slices of smoked mutton and put cabbage on it. Season well with salt, pepper, ground clove and allspice. Just cover with stock and put another layer of sliced smoked mutton on top. Cover and simmer about 1½ hours with a lid on, by which time the liquor should all be absorbed by the cabbage. Remove any whole spices before serving.

Serves 4

SMOKED LAMB WITH MINT CRUST AND WALNUT SAUCE

From Mrs Zandra MacPherson, Glentruin

INGREDIENTS	
4 tsp	Arran mustard
1	leg smoked lamb
175g (6 oz)	breadcrumbs
3 tbs	dried mint
150ml (¼ pt)	red wine
2 tbs	walnut oil
2 tsp	cornflour
150ml (¼ pt)	double cream
1 tbs	chopped walnuts

METHOD

Spread mustard over joint. Mix together breadcrumbs and mint and coat joint. Roast at 190°C, 375°F, Gas Mark 5 for 1½ hours or until cooked. To prepare sauce remove most of fat from roasting tin. Deglaze with red wine. Mix walnut oil and cornflour in a little water and add to roasting tin. As soon as it begins to thicken, add cream and walnuts. Serve with lamb.

Serves 4-6

Salad of Herdwick Macon with Grilled Aubergine and Hummous

From Richard Tonks, Leatham's Larder, London

INGREDIENTS

500g (1 lb)	finely sliced Herdwick macon
3 tbs	olive oil infused with sundried tomatoes
1	medium aubergine
	salt and pepper to taste
	assorted salad leaves
1	lemon
250g (8 oz)	homemade hummous
4 tbs	chopped parsley and chives

METHOD

Liberally brush the macon with the sundried tomato oil and allow to stand. Slice aubergine lengthways into eight, sprinkle with salt and allow to drain in a colander for 30 minutes. Rinse and pat dry thoroughly in a clean tea towel. Brush with the sundried tomato oil and grill until tender and lightly coloured.

Arrange the macon to mostly cover four plates. Dress salad leaves with sundried tomato oil, lemon and salt and pepper to taste. Arrange in centre of plates, with two slices of aubergine per plate, opposite each other. Repeat with dollops of hummous. Sprinkle with herbs.

Serves 4

SMOKED CHEESES

Smoked cheeses pack a wallop of flavour into a small amount of cheese. With cheeses being less dense than meat, the smoke taste really penetrates right through. Cheese lovers will adore them, from smoked Mozzarella, to goats cheese (which can taste like you are standing in a barbecue), to mature Cheddars, to Stilton. It's easy to tell genuinely smoked cheese from smoked-flavour cheese by the marks of the tray the cheese was smoked on; if it has a totally even rind, the smoke is applied externally by a spray. Try wrapping smoked Caerphilly in filo, or adding smoked Cheddar to mashed potatoes.

♀ With cows milk cheeses: Dos Cortados Oloroso by Williams & Humbert and Harvey's 1796 are excellent; Gewurztraminer of Auslese grade; California Merlot; botrytised Semillion/Sauvignon Blanc from Australia; single malt from Speyside.

♀ With goats and sheeps milk cheeses: Rare Oloroso Corregidor sherry by Sandeman; Gewurztraminer of Auslese grade; botrytised Chardonnay from Australia; California Grenache; single malt from Western Isles.

WHOLEMEAL SMOKED WEDMORE CHEESE, LEEK AND POTATO PIE

From Caroline Shoebridge, chef, The Star Inn, Sulgrave, Oxon.

INGREDIENTS

PASTRY

350g (12 oz)	wholemeal flour
350g (12 oz)	self raising flour
2 tsp	dry mustard powder
350g (12 oz)	margarine
	salt
	water

FILLING

500g (1 lb)	potatoes
750g (1½ lb)	leeks
1	medium onion
150g (6 oz)	smoked Wedmore cheese
3	medium eggs, beaten
	salt and fresh black pepper

METHOD

For the pastry, put flours, salt and mustard powder into a large mixing bowl, add margarine and rub fat into the flour until it resembles fine breadcrumbs. Gradually add enough water to form a dough that leaves the bowl cleanly. This can also be done in a food processor. Leave to rest in the refrigerator.

For the filling, peel and dice the potatoes, bring to the boil and par cook for about 5 minutes. Drain. Sauté the leeks and onions in a little butter until soft. Grate the Wedmore cheese with the rind removed. Mix with the other ingredients including most of the beaten egg.

Lightly grease a 23cm (9") tin with a loose base and

line with ⅔ of the pastry. Add the cheese mixture and cover with the remaining pastry. Seal and decorate with scraps of pastry and brush with the reserved beaten egg.

Pierce the centre of the lid and cook in the oven at 190°C, 375°F, Gas Mark 5 for approximately 45 minutes. Serve with salad or seasonal vegetables.

Serves 8 for lunch

CRISPY SMOKED GOATS CHEESE BEIGNETS WITH SALSA AND ASPARAGUS TIPS

From Adam Saville, chef, Cricklade Hotel and Country Club, Cricklade, Wilts.

INGREDIENTS

SALSA

1x400g (14 oz)	tin plum tomatoes, chopped
1	small onion, minced
1	clove garlic, finely minced
3	jalapeño chillies
juice of 1	lime
juice of ½	lemon
	handful of fresh coriander, chopped
2 tsp	olive oil
	salt, fresh ground pepper and pinch of paprika

BATTER

125g (4 oz)	plain flour
5 tbs	cornflour
½ tsp	baking powder
250ml (8 fl.oz)	cold water
½ tsp	salt
1 tbs	extra virgin olive oil

1	raw beetroot
	vegetable oil for deep frying
12	asparagus tips, cut lengthways
2 x 125g (4 oz)	smoked goats cheese
	mixed salad leaves
	flour seasoned with salt and
	pepper for dredging

METHOD

To make salsa, combine all ingredients and season to taste. Allow to stand for 1 hour.

To make batter, mix flour, cornflour and baking powder in bowl. Add water, whisk to a smooth paste. Just before using, whisk in salt and olive oil.

Preheat oil to 180°C, 350°F in a deep fryer.

Peel and very finely slice beetroot, pat dry with kitchen paper and deep fry 1 minute. Drain on kitchen paper and season.

Blanch asparagus for 1 minute in boiling salted water. Drain and keep warm.

Cut each goats cheese into 6 wedges, dredge in seasoned flour, dip into finished batter, deep fry 4 minutes or until crisp and golden. Drain on kitchen paper.

Place three spoonfuls of salsa around plate, place asparagus in between. Arrange beignets on salsa with a few salad leaves in centre of plate topped with a few beetroot crisps. Serve immediately.

Serves 4

Double Baked Smoked Cheese Soufflé

From Chris Suter, Bishopstrow House, Warminster, Wilts.

INGREDIENTS

25g (1 oz)	butter
25g (1 oz)	flour
150ml (¼ pt)	milk
150g (5 oz)	smoked cheddar or goats cheese
3	eggs separated plus 2 whites

METHOD

Melt butter, add flour and make roux. Cook for 2 minutes but do not allow to colour. Gradually stir in milk to make a smooth sauce.

Add 75g (3 oz) cheese and stir until melted. Mixture should be smooth. Remove from heat. Cool slightly and add egg yolks, one at a time.

Whisk whites with pinch of salt until soft peaks form. Add 1 ladle of whites to cheese mixture and whisk in. Then carefully fold in rest of whites.

Butter and flour individual ramekins. Divide mixture among them and bake at 160°C, 325°F, Gas Mark 3 in *bain marie* for 12 minutes.

Tip out while still warm (recipe can be made up to 12 hours in advance at this point). Place soufflés in earthenware dish. Bake at 190°C, 375°F, Gas Mark 5 for 7-8 minutes. Sprinkle with rest of cheese and serve.

Serves 4 - 6

SMOKED MUSHROOMS

Logically speaking, smoked mushrooms should be impossible to produce because of their extremely high water content, which is about 98%. The trick is in careful, cold smoking at about 22°C (72°F), which means that in very warm weather they cannot be made at all. The smoking process reduces their water content by about 25%, concentrating the flavour they already have, and adds an earthy, smoked taste besides. They can be eaten raw in salads and bacon and avocado comes to mind as a particularly good combination. Fill the flat caps with olive tapenade and bake for canapes. Use them in chasseur or cacciatore sauces with chicken or rabbit. Use them in omelettes or frittatas, or in wine sauces for beef and game. As they have so much more flavour than ordinary white mushrooms, you could use them in any recipe that calls for the richer taste of wild mushrooms at a considerably lower price.

SMOKED MUSHROOM AND SMOKED CHEDDAR RISOTTO

From Chris Suter, Bishopstrow House, Warminster, Wilts.

INGREDIENTS	
1	large onion, chopped
1	clove garlic, finely chopped
125g (4 oz)	butter
175g (6 oz)	smoked flat mushrooms, chopped
125g (4 oz)	oyster mushrooms, chopped (or use wild if available)
250g (8 oz)	Arborio rice
½	glass white wine
1.3 litres (2 ¼ pt)	light chicken or vegetable stock, hot
175g (6 oz)	grated smoked cheddar cheese
	salt and pepper
	fresh thyme, sage or parsley
1 tsp	olive oil

Sweat onion and garlic in butter, uncovered. Add mushrooms and cook 2 minutes.

Add rice and cook another 2 minutes then add white wine and reduce.

Add about 300ml ($\frac{1}{2}$ pt) of stock. Cook and stir on gentle heat.

Add stock gradually whenever liquid evaporates. It should all be added in 2 or 3 stages. Continue to cook and stir on gentle heat.Check for seasoning. Rice should be just *al dente*. Stir in 125g (4 oz) of the cheese.

Ladle into bowls and top with the rest of cheese and glaze under the grill. Garnish with herbs and a few drops of olive oil.

Serves 4-6

SMOKED GARLIC

Smoked garlic is making its way into many supermarkets. The flavour becomes quite pronounced if you bake the whole heads in the oven, wrapped in foil, for about an hour. The resulting paste is wonderfully sweet and smoky and would be terrific along with roasts. It's also good in mashed potatoes and is wonderful as an hors d'oeuvre smeared on croûtons, topped with smoked goats cheese and a bit of black olive, briefly heated in the oven. Or try a bit of smoked garlic with roasted new potatoes and fresh rosemary. Use it to make garlic butter and flavour jacket potatoes, mushrooms or baked sweetcorn.

SMOKED NUTS

Smoked almonds and cashews are about the only readily available smoked nuts. I haven't yet encountered smoked brazils, walnuts, cob nuts or peanuts (which are not strictly a nut at all). Smoked almonds and cashews are terrific as snacks and smoked almonds go especially well with a cold glass of dry Fino or Manzanilla sherry. They're useful in salads, stir frys, stuffings and sauces. As nuts are only a small component of most recipes, smoked nuts are a good way to introduce a surprising, smoky note of flavour.

SUPPLIERS DIRECTORY

All producers' and suppliers' products listed are traditionally smoked using hardwoods. Products underlined in an entry are a specialty of the smoker/supplier, or are an especially good example of the item.

ENGLAND

Astwood Village Smokery
Swan Cottage, Astwood
Bucks MK16 9JS
01234 391523

Products: chicken, poussin, pheasant, turkey, duck, goose, sausages, beef, pork, venison, lamb, quail, guinea fowl, fish.

Brown & Forest
Thorney, Longport
Somerset TA10 0DR
01458 251520

Products: eel, salmon, trout, duck, pork.

Butley Orford Oysterage
Market Hill
Orford, Woodbridge
Suffolk IP12 2LH
01394 450322

Products: salmon, trout, cods roe, kippers, bloaters, mackerel, eel.

Cley Smokehouse
Cley, Holt
Norfolk NR25 7RF
01263 740282

Products: kippers, bloaters, salmon

Kingcob Garlic
Langbridge Farm
Newchurch, Sandown
Isle of Wight PO36 0NR
01983 865378

Products: garlic, garlic butter.

The Old Smokehouse
Brougham Hall, Brougham
Penrith
Cumbria CA10 2DE
01768 867772

Products: char, trout, chicken, duck, guinea fowl, goose, pheasant, quail, pork, lamb, sausages, cheddar, goats cheese, Stilton.

Mere Fish Farm
Ivymead, Mere
Warminster, Wilts
BA12 6EN
01747 860461

Products: hot and cold smoked trout, smoked trout terrine.

Minola Smoked Products
Kencot Hill Farmhouse
Filkins, Lechlade
Gloucestershire
GL7 3QY
01367 860391

Products: salmon, New Zealand green-lipped mussels, scallops, prawns, oysters, trout, haddock, "Arbroath-type" haddock, kippers, "Buckling" herrings, "Bloater" herrings, cods roe, chicken, turkey, duck, goose, pigeon, quail, gammon, bacon, venison, beef, lamb, quails eggs, butter, goats cheese, Chewton Mendip cheddar, nuts, foie gras, duck stock and duck fat.

Richardson's Smokehouse
The Old Smokehouse
Bakers Lane
Orford
Suffolk IP12 2LH
01394 450103

Products: pigeon, duck, chicken, pheasant, prawns, cheeses.

The Teesdale Trencherman
Starforth Hall
Barnard Castle
County Durham
DL12 9RA
01833 38370

Products: Herdwick Macon, grouse, beef, bacon, ham, sausage, turkey, pheasant, wild salmon, mackerel, haddock, kippers, quails eggs, cheddar.

The Valley Smokehouse
Elton Farm
Old Wells Road
Dundry nr. Bristol
BS18 8NQ
0117 963 6979

Products: farmed & wild salmon, trout, halibut, sprats, sardines, monkfish, scallops, chicken, duck, turkey, quail, poussin, pigeon, venison, pork, ham, sausages, foie gras, garlic, cheddar.

The Weald Smokery
Mount Farm
Flimwell
East Sussex TN5 7QL
01580 879601

Products: salmon, trout, eel, mussels, haddock, chicken, duck, ham, sausages.

Alan & Day
Unit 2
Toulmin Street
London SE1 1PP
0171 407 0247

Products: kippers, salmon, trout, cods roe, eel, mackerel, halibut, quails eggs.

Harrods
Knightsbridge
London
SW1X 7XL
0171 730 1234

Products: extensive range of smoked fish and meat.

Harvey Nichols
Knightsbridge
London
SW1
0171 235 5000

Products: extensive range of smoked fish and meat.

Oak Lodge Salmon Ltd
The Lodge
24-26 Eastbury Road
London Industrial Park
London E6 4LP
0171 511 2323

*Products: salmon, salmon trout,
trout, halibut, cods roe, tuna, eel.*

Olsen Wine Shippers
Roxby Place
London SW6 1RS
0171 610 2829

*Products: the range of Tombuie
Oak Smoked produce.*

Selfridge's
Oxford Street
London W1A 1AB
0171 629 1234

*Products: extensive range of
smoked fish.*

WALES

Rhydlewis Trout Farm
Rhydlewis, Llandysul
Dyfed SA44 5QS
01239 851224

Products: trout, salmon.

SCOTLAND

The Colfin Smokehouse
Portpatrick, Wigstownshire
Dumfries & Galloway
DG9 9BN
01776 820622

*Products: whisky-barrel oak-
cured salmon, kippers, trout,
mussels, chicken, pheasant, venison.*

Deeside Smoked Salmon
Headinch House
Dinnet, Aboyne
Aberdeenshire
Grampian AB34 5NY
013398 85304

Products: salmon.
Fletchers Fine Foods
Reediehill Farm
Auchtermuchty
Fife KY14 7HS
01337 828369

Products: venison.

The Galloway Smokehouse
Carsluith, Newton Stewart
Dumfries & Galloway
DG8 7DN
01671 820354

*Products: whisky-oak smoked
salmon, venison, chicken, duck,
prawns, eel.*

Game Fayre Ltd
Unit 1
Tayview Industrial Estate
Friarton Road
Perth
Perthshire PH2 8DJ
01738 443200

*Products: Venison, venison
sausages, pheasant, duck, pigeon,
salmon.*

House of Hamilton
Westfield House
By Harburn
West Lothian
EH55 8RB
01506 418434

Products: salmon, wild boar.

Inverawe Smokehouses
Inverawe House
Taynuilt
Argyll PA35 1HU
01866 822446

*Products: trout, salmon, eel,
halibut, kippers, cods roe,
venison, ham, beef, duck, cheddar.*

Loch Fyne Oysters Ltd
Clachan Farm
Ardkinglas, Cairndow
Argyll PA26 8BH
01499 600264

*Products: salmon, kinglas fillet
(centre filet of salmon), eel, cods
roe, trout, mussels, kippers.*

Mermaid Fish Supplies
Clachan, Locheport
Lochmaddy, North Uist
Highlands & Islands
PA82 5ET
01876 580209

*Products: peat-smoked salmon,
cod, whiting, haddock.*

Osprey Seafoods
Inverness
Scotland
01463 790770

*Products: <u>king scallops</u>, whisky
cask/beech smoked salmon, peat
smoked salmon, oysters, mussels.*

The Shetland Smokehouse
Skeld
Shetland Islands ZE2 9NS
01595 860251

*Products: salmon, sea trout,
kippers, mackerel, haddock, cod.*

R.R. Spink & Sons
33-35 Seagate
Arbroath
Angus
Tayside DD11 1BJ
01241 872023

*Products: <u>Arbroath smokies</u>,
salmon.*

Summer Isles Foods
Achiltibuie
Ullapool
Rosshire IV26 2YG
01854 622353

*Products: salmon, Glen Moray
whisky-cure salmon, sea loch
trout, eel, kippers, chicken, duck,
venison, beef, cheddar.*

The Teviot Game Fare
Smokery
Kirkbank House
Eckford, Kelso
Roxburghshire TD5 8LE
01835 850253

*Products: pheasant, chicken,
salmon, trout, eel, cheddar.*

Tombuie Smokehouse
Aberfeldy
Perthshire PH15 2JS
01887 820127

*Products: <u>leg of lamb, guinea
fowl, ham, jambon</u>, venison,
duck, chicken, turkey, quail,
salmon, cheese.*